Exploring World Cultures

Ethiopia

By Nancy DiStasio

Cavendish
Square

New York

Published in 2022 by Cavendish Square Publishing, LLC
243 5th Avenue, Suite 136, New York, NY 10016

Copyright © 2022 by Cavendish Square Publishing, LLC

First Edition

Website: cavendishsq.com

Library of Congress Cataloging-in-Publication Data

Names: DiStasio, Nancy, author.
Title: Ethiopia / Nancy DiStasio.
Other titles: Exploring world cultures.
Description: First edition. | New York : Cavendish Square Publishing, 2022.
| Series: Exploring world cultures | Includes index.
Identifiers: LCCN 2020039595 | ISBN 9781502659002 (library binding) | ISBN
9781502658982 (paperback) | ISBN 9781502658999 (set) | ISBN
9781502659019 (ebook)
Subjects: LCSH: Ethiopia--Juvenile literature.
Classification: LCC DT373 .D57 2022 | DDC 963--dc23
LC record available at https://lccn.loc.gov/2020039595

Editor: Katie Kawa
Copy Editor: Nicole Horning
Designer: Jessica Nevins

Find us on

Contents

The Federal Democratic Republic of Ethiopia is a nation in Africa. Ethiopia is one of the oldest countries in the world. There are around 110 million people living there today, and the population continues to grow.

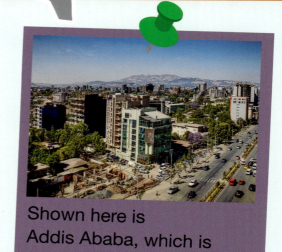

Shown here is Addis Ababa, which is Ethiopia's capital city.

People in Ethiopia are hardworking, but **poverty** is still a big problem in this country. Many Ethiopians live in the countryside, or rural areas. They make their living on farms, growing crops or raising animals. Others live in cities. They work in restaurants, schools, hospitals, or factories.

Ethiopia is a diverse country—home to different groups of people and different kinds of landscapes. Ethiopia has some of Africa's tallest mountains, as well as areas that are below sea level. Some parts of the country are deserts, while others are forests.

Ethiopians speak different languages and follow different religions, or belief systems. Although their lives aren't always easy and their country has

The colors of Ethiopia's flag stand for hope, peace, and heroism.

faced hard times, they still celebrate, or honor, the good things around them.

Ethiopia is a landlocked country, meaning there are no oceans around its borders. It's surrounded instead by countries: Eritrea, Djibouti, Somalia, Kenya, South Sudan,

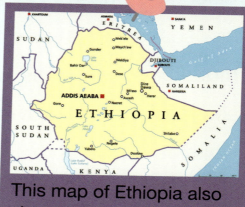

This map of Ethiopia also shows the countries that surround it.

and Sudan. Ethiopia is located in a part of eastern Africa known as the Horn of Africa.

Ethiopia's landscape includes mountains and a plateau—an area of high, flat land. It also includes lowlands that sit below sea level. The East African Rift System, which includes the

FACT!

Ethiopia has a higher population than any other landlocked country on Earth.

Great Rift Valley, cuts through Ethiopia. It's made up of many trenches, or deep and narrow cuts in Earth's surface.

Ethiopia has rivers and lakes, as well as dry deserts. Rainfall in Ethiopia comes in seasons, with periods of wet and dry weather coming at different times of the year.

The East African Rift is home to many volcanoes, such as the one shown here. Many earthquakes, which happen when the ground shakes, also happen in this area.

What Causes a Rift?

The East African Rift was created by the movement of tectonic plates. These are the large pieces of rock that sit on Earth's surface. Their movement can make mountains and valleys, as well as cause earthquakes.

History

Historians believe that what's now Ethiopia was home to early humanlike creatures and some of the first humans. Over time, these early groups of people began to settle and

Shown here is the town of Aksum, where visitors can see things left behind by early Ethiopians.

grow food. Around 100 CE, the powerful kingdom of Aksum began to rule from today's Ethiopia.

Throughout history, outsiders tried to control Ethiopia, but they were mostly unsuccessful. From 1936 to 1941, Italy controlled Ethiopia, but it then stood on its own once again.

Haile Selassie I ruled Ethiopia as emperor from 1930 until he was forced from office in 1974.

8

In 1974, pieces of bones were found in Ethiopia. Scientists believe they came from an early humanlike creature that lived around 3 million years ago! They called the skeleton they built with the bones Lucy.

Ethiopia was ruled by **emperors** for many years. In 1995, Ethiopia's new **constitution** went into effect and set up a more democratic government. People had a bigger say and voted in elections.

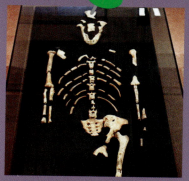

The skeleton of Lucy, which can be seen here, has taught scientists a lot about where humans might have come from.

The border between Ethiopia and Eritrea was fought over for many years. In 2018, the border dispute, or fight, finally came to an end.

VOTE ✔

Ethiopia is one of the oldest independent countries in the world, but its central government has changed a lot over time. Today, it has three branches—much like the government of the United

Prime Minister Abiy Ahmed Ali won the Nobel Peace Prize in 2019 for his actions toward peace with Eritrea.

States. The Ethiopian government is centered in the capital, Addis Ababa.

The legislative branch, or parliament, makes the laws. The executive branch includes

FACT!

Ethiopians can vote when they turn 18 years old.

In 2018, Sahle-Work Zewde became Ethiopia's first female president. The president isn't elected by the Ethiopian people. Instead, Ethiopians elect members of the legislative branch, who then choose the president.

a president, who serves as the head of state. This means they represent, or stand for, Ethiopia on the world stage. However, the prime minister is the main leader of the government.

Sahle-Work Zewde— Ethiopia's first female president—is shown here.

There are also courts, with judges who serve until they are 60 years old. The courts make up the judicial branch of the Ethiopian government.

The Economy

The Ethiopian economy—
its system of making,
buying, and selling
goods—depends heavily
on agriculture, or farming.
People who live in the
country are mainly

The birr is Ethiopia's basic **unit** of money.

farmers. However, it's sometimes hard to grow crops.
The soil can be poor. Droughts, or periods of little or
no rain, will slow or stop plant growth. Some areas
of the country produce good crops, including grains,
coffee, and vegetables. Farmers in Ethiopia also raise
animals, such as cattle.

FACT!

The Ethiopian government controls all the
land in the country.

Coffee as a Cash Crop

Coffee is Ethiopia's most important export, or good sold to other countries. Ethiopia is known as one of the first places in the world where coffee beans grew.

There are different jobs for people who live in Ethiopia's cities. Some have service jobs, such as jobs in hospitals or hotels. Factory workers make clothing and other goods.

This Ethiopian woman is drying coffee beans to sell.

Many Ethiopians live in poverty. Although many efforts are being made to boost the Ethiopian economy, it's still one of the poorest countries in the world.

13

The Environment

Ethiopia has many beautiful natural landscapes—from the mountains to the savanna, or grassland. It's home to many popular animals, such as lions, elephants, and giraffes.

Shown here is the Ethiopian wolf. It's one of many animals in Ethiopia in danger of dying out.

However, Ethiopia also has many environmental problems, or problems dealing with the natural world. Many Ethiopians are living without **access** to clean, safe drinking water.

FACT!

Deforestation, or the cutting down of trees, is harming the environment in Ethiopia.

Water from rivers can be dirty and make people sick. In some places, people need to walk a long way to get water to drink.

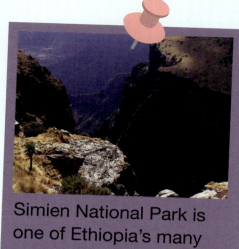

Simien National Park is one of Ethiopia's many national parks.

In 2015, Ethiopia began a period of terrible drought. The lack of rain led to poor crop growth and limited water for drinking. In 2020, locusts attacked parts of the country. These bugs destroyed crops and pushed people from their homes.

Dealing with Dirt

Farming and human settlement have caused the top **layer** of soil to wear away in some parts of Ethiopia. This makes the soil less fertile, or good for farming.

Today, there are more than 110 million people living in Ethiopia. Only one other country in Africa (Nigeria) has more people living in it. Ethiopia's population is young. About half of

Kids make up a large part of Ethiopia's population.

all Ethiopians are children or teenagers. Ethiopia's population is also growing quickly, and women in this country often have many children. This can make it hard for families to get enough food and water because there are so few **resources** for so many people.

FACT!

Some Ethiopians have immigrated, or moved, to other countries, such as the United States.

Ethiopians don't pass down last names. At birth, Ethiopian children are given a first name, and their father's name becomes their last name.

Ethiopia is made up of around 80 different ethnic groups. Many Ethiopians belong to the Oromo, Amhara, Tigray, and Somali ethnic groups. Ethnic groups unite people based on common **traits**, often including language.

Most Ethiopians live in rural areas. However, the capital city of Addis Ababa is home to more than 4 million people.

Markets such as this one are common places for Ethiopians to gather.

17

Around 80 percent of Ethiopians live outside the country's major cities. **Paved** roads aren't always found in rural areas, so people get around by walking or riding animals. Homes

In Ethiopia, it's often a woman's job to carry water or wood for a fire back to her family's home.

in rural Ethiopia are simple. Some are built from wood and mud. Others are made from stone.

Some Ethiopians leave the countryside to try to build a better life in a city. They hope to make

FACT!

Older people hold a high place of honor in Ethiopia.

18

more money and go to better schools. Many cities in Ethiopia offer higher paying jobs, cleaner water, and electricity, which rural areas often don't have.

These Ethiopian students are learning English.

Many Ethiopian children are busy helping on farms or taking care of younger siblings. This makes it hard for them to finish school. Only about half of adult Ethiopians can read and write.

A Deadly Sickness

A sickness known as HIV, which can lead to a deadly health problem known as AIDS, is a big problem in Africa, including in Ethiopia. Doctors from around the world are working to keep Ethiopians from getting this sickness.

Religion

More than 65 percent of Ethiopians are followers of a Christian religion. The Ethiopian Orthodox Tewahedo Church is the branch of Christianity with the most followers in

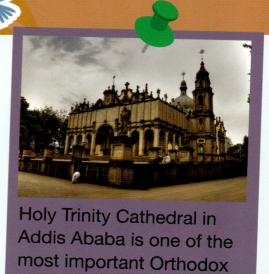

Holy Trinity Cathedral in Addis Ababa is one of the most important Orthodox churches in Ethiopia.

this country. Other Ethiopian Christians are Roman Catholics or Protestants. Christians follow the teachings of Jesus Christ. Important holidays they celebrate include Christmas and Easter.

FACT!

The Ethiopian Orthodox Tewahedo Church is part of a branch of Christianity called Oriental Orthodox Churches.

Animism

A small number of Ethiopians follow a belief system called animism. Animists believe all things, including parts of the natural world and man-made objects, have a spirit.

About 31 percent of the Ethiopian population is Muslim. They follow the teachings of Muhammad. There are smaller groups of people who practice other

These Muslim men are praying together in Ethiopia.

religions. However, many Ethiopians who practiced Judaism moved to Israel.

Some Ethiopians practice traditional African religions—ones that have been passed down over many years. These religions existed long before Christianity came to Ethiopia.

Language

Ethiopia is a land of many languages. An Ethiopian's ethnic background and location plays a part in the language they speak. Oromo is the most common language

Ethiopian students sometimes practice the Amharic language in school.

spoken in Ethiopia, but Amharic is often called the country's official language. Although the government officially recognizes all Ethiopian languages, Amharic is known as the "working language" of the government.

FACT!

Almost 30 percent of Ethiopians speak a language called Somali.

The Amharic Language

The Amharic language uses a writing system called *Fidel*. Each character stands for a consonant and a vowel used together.

Ge'ez is a very old language from the past that's still part of life for some Ethiopians. The Ethiopian Orthodox Tewahedo Church still uses Ge'ez in its rituals, or religious events, and its writings.

This Ethiopian Orthodox priest is showing an example of religious writings done in Ge'ez.

Many Ethiopians speak more than one language. Children who attend school learn English. This makes it one of the most popular foreign, or outside, languages in Ethiopia.

Music is an important part of life in Ethiopia. Many Ethiopian musicians use traditional instruments to play traditional songs. Brass bands have also become popular in this country over the years.

Many of the paintings found in Ethiopia are religious, such as this artwork found in an old church.

Ethiopians also perform, or take part in, plays. There are theater festivals, or gatherings, in Ethiopia where many plays are performed for the public.

FACT!

The Ethiopian National Theatre is located in Addis Ababa.

Many other Ethiopian festivals are based on religion. Timket, or the Feast of Epiphany, is celebrated in January by members of the Ethiopian Orthodox

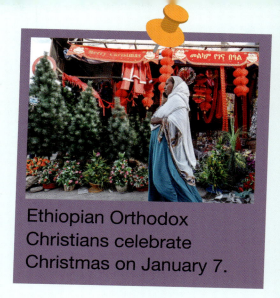

Ethiopian Orthodox Christians celebrate Christmas on January 7.

Tewahedo Church. It honors the baptism of Jesus, which is when he was washed in the Jordan River before starting his preaching. Meskel takes place at the end of September. It celebrates the finding of the cross that Jesus died on.

Ethiopian New Year

Ethiopians celebrate the New Year on September 11, according to the calendar used in the United States. People sing and dance, and gifts of flowers and cards are given.

As in other countries, Ethiopian children enjoy playing games. Some popular ones include a board game called *gebeta* and *segno maksegno*, which is their form of hopscotch. *Yegena chewata* is like field hockey and is commonly played around Christmas. Ethiopians often play this game with homemade sticks and balls.

Ethiopians, especially young girls, often jump rope for fun.

Running is a big part of the Ethiopian culture,

Ethiopians played a big part in making soccer (or football) more popular in Africa.

Learning About History

Ethiopia has a rich history. People can visit museums, especially in Addis Ababa, to learn more about this history. Museums are places where objects of historical, cultural, and artistic importance are kept and shown.

or way of life. Ethiopia produces some of the fastest runners in the world! About 40,000 people run the Great Ethiopian Run every year. It takes place in Addis Ababa. Runners in this 10K (about 6 miles) race include famous Ethiopian runners and visitors from all over the world.

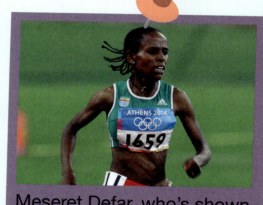

Meseret Defar, who's shown here, is one of Ethiopia's most famous female runners.

Ethiopian food has bold and spicy flavors. A traditional stew, called *wat* (or *wot*), can be made from meats, vegetables, or beans. It's often made spicy

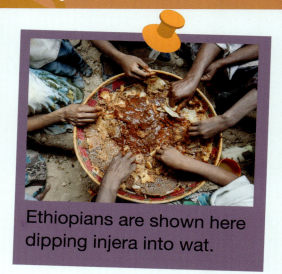

Ethiopians are shown here dipping injera into wat.

with berbere, which is a spice mix with dried red chili peppers. A serving plate is often lined with injera, a flat bread that looks like a thin pancake. People tear off injera pieces and use them instead of forks or spoons to eat the stew. They only use

FACT!

Italy's period of control over Ethiopia helped pasta become a popular food in this country.

Ethiopians sometimes feed each other pieces of injera or a spoonful of wat. This practice, called *gursha*, is used to show love and caring.

their right hand to pick up food and eat.

Ethiopia is believed to be the birthplace of coffee. People roast coffee beans over a fire. Then, they grind, or crush, the beans and **brew** the tasty drink. Tea is another popular drink among Ethiopians.

Ethiopian women prepare and serve coffee in a special way, called a coffee ceremony.

Glossary

access   The ability to use or have something.

brew   To make a drink using hot water.

constitution The basic laws by which a country, state, or group is governed.

emperor   A ruler of an empire who often rules with total control.

layer   One part of something lying over or under another.

pave   To cover the ground with a material, such as tar or concrete, that forms a hard, level surface for walking and driving.

poverty   The state of being poor.

resource   Something that can be used.

trait   A quality that makes one person or thing different from another.

unit   A particular amount of something, such as money, that is used as a standard for counting or measuring.

Find Out More

Books

Brinker, Spencer. *Ethiopia*. Minneapolis, MN: Bearport
    Publishing, 2018.

Gale, Ryan. *Your Passport to Ethiopia*. North
    Mankato, MN: Capstone Press, 2021.

Website

Britannica Kids: Ethiopia

kids.britannica.com/kids/article/Ethiopia/345687

This website features pictures, videos, and details
about the people and culture of Ethiopia.

Video

Go on a Journey with an Ethiopian Wolf Family

www.youtube.com/watch?v=ROU7vh2QJTM&t=10s

This *National Geographic* video shows how the
Ethiopian wolf hunts for its food and lives in the wild.

Index

About the Author

Nancy DiStasio loves learning and teaching others about world cultures. As a librarian, she helps people find information they need. She enjoys eating authentic Ethiopian food in her hometown, located in Western New York.